Wake the Stars

GW00362072

Poems and Ly

Laurence McPartlin

ISBN: 978-1-9996359-1-6

Collingwood
Publishing & Media

For Beverley, Ben and Rory

TABLE OF CONTENTS

	Acknowledgments and Foreword	6-7
1	In the Silence of Time	9
2	Wake the Stars	10
3	What is this Grief if not Eternity?	11
4	The Girl who Lives by the Sea	12
5	Liz	14
6	Resting at Kirkstone Pass	15
7	Lust Sent me Sleep	16
8	Dalton Beck	18
9	Cry Earth	20
10	The Sky is falling…and…	21
11	In my Love	22
12	Bridge of Light	24
13	White Horses	26
14	Storm Running	27
15	Catch Me if you Can	28
16	Lochinvar Summer of 76	29
17	Tears of Venus	31
18	Oradour-sur-Glane	32
19	Sketching by the River	33
20	131 Dunbar Road	34

21	Steelworks	35
22	Cockleridge	36
23	Shine	37
24	Mountains in the Clouds	38
25	Spain	39
26	Not Far from Hawes	41
27	Suilven	42
28	In the Blind Garden	43
29	Girl in the Café	45
30	Reeth to Keld	46
31	Planet Waves	48
32	Witness	49
33	School Friends	50
34	Seaton Carew	51
35	Friendship	52
36	Hartlepool	53
37	River Erme	55
38	Bruises	57
39	Sea of Sleep	58
40	Erin and Libby – Kisses for Free	60
	About the Author	61

To Quiel

all the Best

[signature]

ACKNOWLEDGMENTS

I owe a great debt of gratitude to many friends, including my editor, John Simes, for his patient deciphering of my wayward handwriting, and skillful crafting of my work. Thanks also to Jo Simes for her support and encouragement. Thanks to Lisa Dyer for the brilliant cover photography. I also had the support of a wonderful team of listeners and readers – David Holland, Matthew and Kate Holland, Gary and Michele Blampied, and Teresa Clark.

"He who kisses joy as it flies by will live in eternity's sunrise." – William Blake

Foreword

The joy of editing Laurence McPartlin's poems is to become a companion, a fellow traveller on that wayward pathway from youth to maturity and beyond. It is not a solemn walk, but one of curiosity, deriving joy and understanding from every blade of grass, from the mountainous Kirkstone Pass in Cumbria, the tumbling streams of Dalton Beck to the spaces and majesty of Spain and its never-ending skies.

Mac's work, imbued by the rhythms of folk and dance, have a music that evokes the Chartist movement of the 1830s to the 1850s, spanning the ages of Romanticism and Pre-Raphaelite art and poetry. The work of Southey, Hogg and Bloomfield sits well with Mac's talent for vivid vignettes and vibrant detail. Throughout these poems there is light, a youthful mind never resting but – as in Steelworks – plotting its escape from darkness; and doing it with a zeal and wicked ebullience that charms the reader.

In 'Catch Me If You Can', the wilful child has become a man for whom 'pearl shell comets are the only wings I need'. Figures dance and play throughout the poems, the worker, the jester, the minstrel, and images of children that recall the *Echoing Green* and the *Songs of Innocence* by William Blake.

So, join us on this walk through McPartlin's life. Bring your sketchbook and pencils, and that guitar and, yes, those eyes. But do as he does. Take your time, spend aeons of it, watch and learn, be patient as a clock and look deeply into the heart of things.

John Simes

February 23, Challaborough, Devon, UK.

In the Silence of Time

My windows are open,
I can see clouds of
thistledown slowly drifting
west,
peeling back the stars.
The long deep swell of the sea
makes me restless;
I need to lean against
the moon,
and let the hungry
dream shells empty
into my harbour of liquid time,
thirsty and touched with
flame.
How my heart aches,
When I'm sailing in the past, free
In the silence of time.

Wake the Stars

(for Jo and John Simes)

Isn't it a beautiful night
to ring the bells
and wake the stars?
The tide is right, and
the moon is on the
run.
I feel like dancing on sand
And wetting my toes in the sea.
The sky is singing,
soaking my eyelids with
laughter. "Come on, come on!"
it sings! "Climb in!"

What is this Grief if not Eternity?

The grains of life
Have been summoned,
like a silent sea
closing down the years.
And the patterns of
the day are meaningless,
long overdue memories
deliver themselves -
blood veined,
groping for a meaning.
I have no prayers
to offer.
The true grain is
shell wrecked,
A thousand seasons sleeping.
What is this grief,
if not eternity?
The seas of life
will continue
to remember, and I will
carry lanterns whose
blades of light will
give reason
never to forget.

The Girl who Lives by the Sea

Lights from the towers
flicker and die;
the porcelain face sails
through the night,
silhouette people weave and
dissolve like pebbles
washed by the tide.
It's not a long way home,
the dove's voice is silent.

It's been said she writes poetry,
for swollen eyelids in
the rain, for agony and oceans,
mute swans and destiny.
In her fire, dying love is alive,
Unharmed,
and all flowers that wither
in winters grip
She will place beneath the
quiet trees
filling their roots with
secret oils, until they burst
again with colour.

The sea is always waiting, even on a
starless night.

She will sleep with
the window open and
let the waves of the
world continue with
their timeless journey,
and if her dreams are
filled with brine-scented
wrack and babbling ghosts,
She will sing to the moon
and put the stars to bed.

Liz

She was watching,
from her window -
lights across the sea.

"I've seen them before!"
I heard her say,
"Can't catch me!"

"Silly moon. It's very late.
Sleep with me awhile.
We'll chase the lights
another night.
Soon the sun will rise."

"You see I am a child again
and have to close my eyes."

Resting at Kirkstone Pass

I grasped one single blade
of grass, so wild,
so smooth and free.
I cast it to the mellow
wind,
and away it blew from me.

In my fingertips, I held one
twig then
turned it slowly round.
I placed it among wild heather,
where beauty made no sound.

One piece of fern lay
on my palms -
so rough,
yet silently warm.
I placed it on a stony mound
To be kissed by the sun at dawn.

Lust Sent me to Sleep

We met when we were young,
in a room where rumours
had captured my attention.
You, deep in thought, were
somewhere else.

I was like a pauper,
condemned to the night's embrace
without a compass, powerless to
lure a single star to steer me.

Love's freedom meant something
that night.
I left the window open,
illuminated by the street
light.

I felt the ways of the world
shudder and take possession of my
heart, sweating
like an open flower.

In this landscape of sailing moons
and ripened dreams,
you gave me everything,
generous and passionate.

Filling me with night fever
in a ballad of breathless glory.

Lust send me to sleep,
Deprived of nothing.

Dalton Beck

All on a summers day
at Dalton Beck,
wrapped up in colours,
laughing
we chased sticklebacks
and minnows with tiny
nets. Our eyes wide like
hungry slaves searching
the waters' pulse.

We ran, as wild horses down
sun-baked slopes,
scattering insects through
trees of shimmering light.

Just a bunch of scruffy
runaways with chains
of buttercups and roots,
stumbling and slipping
on moss covered stones,
in perfect pandemonium.

Hurling ourselves through
Hedgerows, grabbing handfuls
of hickory dock, gasping
like frogs, looking like scarecrows.

Down lanes, overflowing
with crowds of dandelions,
kissed by butterflies, we
rolled like waves, smashing
the cloudless sky and with
pockets filled with ants and
muck, we climbed gates of
rotten wood trembling like
acrobats, faces red as plums.

Under the bridge we
raced bits of wood
round rocks and watercress,
then crawled under fences
stuffed with nettle and
thorn, flushing out birds
some the colour of rainbows
captured by the sun.
The green meadow sang,
brimming with blossom.
Snug, as a bed.

For my brother, Stephen

Cry Earth

Take these strings
from my guitar and let her sleep.
The moon is dead,
The sun is dead,
She will sing no more.

Here, among the deepest
wounds,
rivers have been
sentenced to mist and fire;
where once they touched
the singing trees,
and chased each season's melt.

Kill the voices!
Save the souls!
Hold your bloody sacrifice
God's desire, your desire!
Fill the earth with bones!
Earth! Cry, earth!

The Sky is falling...and...

I cannot find my wings today.
My eyes are filled
with winter
Intense with the living past.

Old wounds are silent,
buried somewhere,
splintered, thirsty and treacherous,
like quicksand.

Each blood drained vision
struggles to make sense.

Why men must die on battlefields
for peace?

So many flowers call upon me. They say,
"Do not forsake my world's tread!
Do not consume yourself with
farewells! Find your light.
Fly again."

In my Love

In my love, *you* are my love!
Silver moon, enchant.
Declare your passion.
You *are* my love -
sweet scented caravans sail through
the night
and come to open pathways where
flowers shine,
leaving kisses for me to follow
in a thirsty landscape.

In the ripe morning,
you are *my* love -
my heart flushed with perfumed
dreams, strays in a garden of
shipwrecked stars.
Fishes play in ribbons of crystal
and shepherds, like captive birds
gather old songs of lavender
and thyme for me
to sing in fountains.

My love – you are my love.
Fields of amber sunflowers shine,
ancient pathways lead me
to the sea. Tiny shells are

singing, calling out to me,
You are my love!

For Beverley

Bridge of Light

Come to me now!
I'm ready to talk.
I can be brief -
stripped to the bone -
if that's all you need.
Let me loosen the
clanking chains.
Already, I'm filled with moon,
Invisible, but in plain view.

I can tell you stories
riddled with dizzying imagery
and shifting fog.
If you look into my eyes
you will see the truth.
What places I could take you -
depending on your nerve!
Far more personal and intimate!
Let us clash like blind ships
and salvage what we can.

Come to me now -
I'm ready to talk.
Some wounds never heal,
when silence keeps you
on the very edge,

impossible to map - until
water droplets gather up
our colours,
and release them from stone.
I'm ready to talk.

White Horses

Great gushing seas,
foaming, crashing!
Sing to me, sing to me,
without rigging or secrets.
A merry dance of prancing dragons.

Diamond voices kiss emeralds,
Laughing -
sing to her, sing to her
in bare feet with passion.
A swirling waltz of lizards and salt.

Bloom, bloom orange moon,
that glitters and wanes.
Sing, sing like fishermen,
ride the silver waves!
Dance, dance in foam and rags -
hang rainbows in the spray.

Great gushing seas!
The fish are caught in
water wheels,
rolling and foaming like
jewels and pearls,
riding white horses.
Flying.

Storm Running

I like it when the east
wind is roaring,
rushing up my sleeves
like a hungry tide.
Strong and piercing,
the Great North Sea smashes
over Longscar rocks and
claws at the harbour walls
in great thunderous bursts,
draining the suns light
- a mocking cloak.

In the distance, St Hilda's
clings to the headland like
a shipwreck.
I can just make out the steeple,
probing the clouds in defiance, and the
pitch fork rain pushes me along
Seaton Carew in a whirlwind,
drenched to the bone, alive
and damned,
reaching into the mutinous
storm, triumphant in the bedlam.

Catch Me if you Can

Catch me if you can,
and colour in my fevered dreams.
I wear a coat of
singing bells, all in silver blue,
that clings to the moon
like a fragile sail
somewhere out at sea.
I'm dancing 'neath the stars,
blowing on the wind;
no harbour to hold me
no tide to lock me in.
The constellations are blind
to my timeless wheels,
and pearl shell comets are
the only wings I need when
I'm travelling like this!

For Ben and Rory

Lochinvar Summer of 76

The leaves on the trees
hang heavy,
smacked down, sulking,
waiting for a rain filled wind
to wet the cruel sun.
Even the birds are silent,
in this landscape of wood and stone.

The Inver slips by,
liquid glass,
everything below revealed and
there - suspended in the depths -
the brown trout is hesitant to rise
and take the fragile wings
that hover above, shimmering
and blind to the hunter's eyes.

Nothing moves,
except the eagle - its
talons hunger to tear flesh,
no mercy for the carcass.
It's good to find shade and
listen to the earth humming,
deep, floating, sensual.

I will not beg for the moon
to release the summer's grip.
Soon enough winter will
have its way,
and paint the colours out.

Tears of Venus

Into the night,
into the frame,
hollow moons and masters,
violins shake the hourglass
like wampum beads
whispering secrets,
beyond the blessed isles.

Into the night,
into the frame,
the great northern lights
dance on my shoulders,
catching the tears of Venus
from horizon to horizon.
The leaves of stars are falling.

Oradour-sur-Glane

When the war is over,
whose corridor will you walk down,
with pages of lies conjured up
in utter faith, to satisfy the living?
There was a time when
none of us could see
how close we were to hell.

Yet, hell itself you brought
and more, without
mercy.
I was glad to be down there
to see, for myself,
how freely you delivered
death's sword to the innocent.
All I could do was weep.

Sketching by the River

I am quiet – like a
loch flattened – who's
waters are content
to let the moon's ladder
reach down
and touch the surface
of her womb.

This is a new experience -
it's almost midnight -
but I'll sketch some more.

Leonard sings Suzanne and
other songs for me,
pouring out his heart.

This is a beautiful hunger
and I'm patient with
my pencil.

Unable to rush the passion
within these walls.

131 Dunbar Road

In the temple of crumpled
gold and luminous thread,
we devoured all we could
to satisfy the howling dogs
of time.

Every night, the thirsty moon
would find us,
leaning on her mantle of glass,
waiting for the stars to fall
like petals -
a thousand kisses singing.

Here we touched comets,
wheeling the infinite
far away from the sun's pulse.
You could lay naked with
Venus or sweat, like a
sulking sea,
with secrets on your lips.

The waves of the world
plucked our strings,
shells broke sand-measured
time, and the dove's voice
gathered up our dreams and
carried them away.

Steelworks

This is a dangerous place.
I will work hard to find
a way out.
Hot steel and long shifts
bind you to this life.
I pretend I'm part of it
while planning my escape.
When the buggers find out
I never joined the union.
They will help me on my way.

They did.

Cockleridge

It's something to do with
being beside the sea.
It holds me like a child,
full of possibilities,
ever changing,
perfect restlessness.
Savaged by storms and
dead calm
- when touched by the moon.
A beautiful place to be
at peace.
With water music,
Breathing.

Shine

Kiss the stars,
blow with the wind,
hang your hat on the moon.
Roam where you will
drink your fill.

Sleep with someone you love,
be an artist,
visual and loud,
love your family,
love your friends.

Say yes to everything.

For Patrik and Karin Reichle, Pleidelsheim, Germany

Mountains in the Clouds

Sitting on a low wall,
aged seven at the
top of Jutland Road.

Watching the storm clouds
roll in from the west,
dark and shaped like
mountains.

I remember thinking
one day I'll go see
for myself what's on
the other side.

That day arrived soon
enough and
I just kept on.
Going.

Spain

Churches and kingdoms
rule this land
of shimmering light -
only the blood truth matters.

Kings and Queens lay silent
in cold stone,
their names etched out to
remind you of the final debt.

The stars in the
constellations - like
bounty hunters running out time,
cultivate silence
when the sun is sleeping.

Poets weep, and ancient walls
whisper of love and hate.
Only the moon and old
paintings witness the truth.
Thousands of voices sing to
the sculptor's hand.

It's better to be expressive,
transparent like the saints
on fragile windows.

This is a place where
gipsies dance
pious and moody, filled
with duande!

Your very soul knows life.
And death.

Not Far from Hawes

The skylark sings above me
where clouds beat like hearts,
far away from the swelling
seas and fishermen.

The rhythm of time has
kept its promise, and
brought me to this place.
Stars and moons
are generous with
their beauty.

I've walked a long way to
know these hills.
Here I am,
on Wether Fell,
not far from Hawes.

Suilven

Loch Fionn sleeps below
me and promises nothing
but silence and truth,
touched only by the passage of time.

Behind me stands Suilven,
drinking the clouds dry,
its belly faces west -
a magnificent beast -
mocking the sun's brilliance.

Old as earth itself,
faithful only to the
constellations, a place
where dreams are wide awake
and all gods are muted.

In the Blind Garden

Tears fill the landscape
where the bone serpent sleeps.
I see you alone on a moonless
sea, clutching at wood and saints.
Waiting, just waiting
like churches do,
for guiltless souls to confess
to marble wings,
plucked like flowers, in
a blind garden.

I hear you in the abyss
talking to ruins and ghosts;
fragments of your childhood
slip in
like sunflowers overlooked,
each petal a suspect
which cannot be opened, while
your lips are numb in
quiet desperation.

Come with me and we'll
sing with fishermen.
They understand the sea -
sometimes it's filled with
thunder claps and fiery suns that bite

stars fall like fabulous pearls -
Catch them if you can!

'Sail again, sail again,' they sing!
Stretch the sun and
put the moon to bed.

Girl in the Café

The sky is singing, rain
soaking my shoes and coat.
What's so bad about that? I
thought artists generally
look like unmade beds.

When I meet her, I'll
sit near the jukebox -
warmest place in the café,
no sense in making a fuss!

Once we get talking
we're anchored in our own
little harbour, sloshing around
courtship like cooing pigeons.

I love her dirty smile. It
fuses me like a firework
and fills my head with naked
thoughts, foamed and weightless,
leaving my eyes glazed and
toes dancing.

Needing no persuasion.

Reeth to Keld

The early morning sun soaks
through the hedgerows,
filling my path with dancing
light, dreaming me along
westward towards Keld -
silently and unseen,
touched only by a warm breeze,
harmonious and fleeting.

I left Reeth some time ago
with it's whispering cottages
and ribbons of stone that
reach deep into the valley
and beyond,
like a serpent sleeping,
breathing its own melody.

The river Swale cools my
feet, where tiny fishes
shimmer in the water music,
elusive and sublime.

It's good to sit like this
and let the landscape come
to me.

When I make my way
through Muker and Thwaite.

Time will follow me,
humming gently.

Planet Waves

Kisses of the moon
touch my fingers,
moving them up and
down like a restless
wind - impossible to
predict.

Freedom comes without
warning - flint sharp
and trembling.

She's locked in the earth's
pulse, dancing me madly
like a sweating sea - and
won't let go until the
tide is out.

Witness

The chief of police
engraves his name
on the drunkard,
tied to the ring.

Famously, the tiles shine -
a thousand mirrors, watching
in silence.

School Friends

Each time I think of you
my heart swells like the sea.
You come to me in a pool of light
free from the place of dreams.

Once, we were like shooting stars
running down the sky,
again and again.

We followed everything through
till, exhausted like the tide,
anchored to the moon.

The years have slipped by,
my friends.
In the garden of our youth
we were invincible -
free to reach the stars,
oblivious to time's illusion.

Living for the moment,
eager and true,
blowing on the wind,
like skylarks.

In memory of Albert Kidd and Ronald Carter

Seaton Carew

Come with me to the
Sea of postcards -
you don't need tickets
to browse.
The smell of food and
sun tan oil
moves you along with
the crowds.

All of your senses are
kidnapped - a different
programme introduced.
Shops are dressed like
dismantled ships
and your eyelids sweat
like ripe fruit,
revealing all the racked
up possibilities on a
tide of chaos,
leaving you – unmirrored -
against the backdrop of
blue skies and broken shells.

Friendship

When we don't understand a language
we speak, like chattering children do,
with waving hands and dancing eyes!

Until, like birds,
we suddenly burst
into song.

Our unseen hearts are
Revealed,
touched by a wind of light,
and the great distance of silence is
awakened to friendship,
for all the world to see.

For Elfi and Theo Rauwald, Leipzig, Germany

Hartlepool

Gulls cry,
children weep,
mothers trying to make
ends meet.
Porridge for breakfast,
pease pudding for tea
and, a nice
washdown in a lovely
tub with soap hard as brick.
Exquisite – delicious.
Living the dream.

For everyone, the
steelworks thrive;
black smoke hangs
in the air - like
a sea coal tide,
covering my plastic shoes.

Learn to read, learn
to write, school is
full of wonders, and
windows easy for escape!
Exquisite – delicious,
living the dream.

When I get off the bus
Lynn Street is mine!
The indoor market is
where I like to be.
I can fill my mouth
with corn beef slice, washed
down with lemonade.
Bargains here, bargains there -
Sixpence in my pocket!
I can buy the world.

Exquisite – delicious.
Living the dream.

River Erme

What silence snow brings -
thin ice clutches the riverbank,
long fingers stretch deep
into the wood, like flickering tongues.

The pewter sky rubs blades
of mosaic sunlight,
filling the hedgerows with
lustre shells.

I like to be alone in this
landscape and touch the trees
with my cold hands -
speechless.

The river slips by in this
fractured light, deep breathing,
sparking the scenery like a
comets tail.

I feel myself smiling, as voices
Of tiny birds follow me like
curious children, and silver
stars fall like flowers.

It's good,

to witness the beauty of
winters promise.

Bruises

Always a stranger,
Distant,
yet close enough to touch.

I do not mind if you hold
my hand; better
if you held me close -
stop my clock springs
from running away.

Just anchor me for a moment,
and let my tears - just for
once - be of happiness.

Speak my name. Bind your
bandage round my troubled mind.
Help me navigate the silence.

Sea of Sleep

I broke into the desert,
no gems behind the gate.
Just an old man selling wishes
and a young man dealing fate.
"Come on in! The water's fine.
Enter her embrace.
She will be your masterpiece,
you will be a slave!"
Just a little mystery,
Just a little game.

Kiss a fool, polar stars
the tapestry is torn.
Broken wings and offerings
lay scattered on the floor.
"Come on in! The water's fine.
It's the middle of July. But
there's a cold wind blowing.
No place else to hide."

Monuments and sacrifice
abandoned and contrived.
Hold hands with good intentions,
but sleep on different sides.
"Come on in! the water's fine.
She's ready to oblige.

All in good time!
Everything will be revealed."

The white moon is sleepwalking.

Kisses for Free

Kisses for free,
just like sunshine,
make me smile!
Light on the water,
sun is high,
children are playing at the
edge of tide.

We followed the dragon trail
across the sands,
and caught tiny fishes in our hands!
Catch us if you can!

Chasing a butterfly
all white and jade -
it rolled and tumbled
just like a wave.

Kisses for free,
just like sunshine.
make me smile!

For Erin and Libby

About the Author

Laurence McPartlin was born in Hartlepool; after leaving school he worked in the local steelworks, before venturing to a new career at a hotel at Lochinver, Scotland. His travels then took him south to work in hotel management in Harrogate, before finally putting his roots down in the leafy South Hams, Devon, United Kingdom. He enjoys playing the guitar, song writing and sketching.

"You are all welcome to….

Come dance with me
On a pale white shore
To the sound of the crazy sea
Where wild winds take your breath away
And set your spirit free…."

You can find out more about Laurence at Collingwood Publishing and Media Ltd www.johnsimes.co.uk or contact him at: macduck52@icloud.com